Jimmy Carter
For the People

Dona Herweck Rice

Consultants

Regina Holland, Ed.S., *Henry County Schools*
Christina Noblet, Ed.S., *Paulding County*
   School District
Jennifer Troyer, *Paulding County Schools*
Michele M. Celani, M.S.Ed., *Baldwin County*
   Public Schools

Publishing Credits

Rachelle Cracchiolo, M.S.Ed., *Publisher*
Conni Medina, M.A.Ed., *Managing Editor*
Emily R. Smith M.A.Ed., *Series Developer*
Diana Kenney, M.A.Ed., NBCT, *Content Director*
Torrey Maloof, *Editor*
Courtney Patterson, *Multimedia Designer*

Image Credits: Front cover: LOC [LC-DIG-ppmsca-09783]; pp.2, 26-27 Emily Staub/The Carter Center; pp.2, 14 LOC [LC-USZC4-2007]; pp.2,3,6,8,12-13 Jimmy Carter National Historic Site; pp.2,10 LOC [LC-DIG-fsa-8b32081]; p.3 Everett Collection Historical / Alamy Stock Photo; pp.4,7 Corbis; p.5 LC [Survey HABS GA-245]; p.6 Ian Dagnall / Alamy Stock Photo; p.9 Courtesy of National Archives [Identifier: 593560]; pp.11,19-21 Granger, NYC; p.12 Richard Ellis / Alamy Stock Photo, Patti McConville / Alamy Stock Photo; p.14 LOC [pan 6a33202]; p.15 Atlanta Journal-Constitution/AP Images; pp.16-17,24,32 Bettmann/CORBIS; p.18 Hulton Archive/Getty Images; p.22 GL Archive / Alamy Stock Photo; p.23 Everett Collection/Newscom; p.25 ClassicStock / Alamy Stock Photo; p.27 Akademie / Alamy Stock Photo; pp.24-25,27-28 Everett Collection Historical / Alamy Stock Photo; p.29 LOC [cw102260]; p.31 The Carter Center/Knudson Photo.; All other images from Shutterstock.

Library of Congress Cataloging-in-Publication Data

Names: Rice, Dona. author.
Title: Jimmy Carter : for the people / Dona Herweck Rice.
Description: Huntington Beach, CA : Teacher Created Materials, 2016. |
   Includes index. | Audience: Grades K to 3.?
Identifiers: LCCN 2015042500 | ISBN 9781493825615 (pbk.)
Subjects: LCSH: Carter, Jimmy, 1924---Juvenile literature. |
   Presidents--United States--Biography--Juvenile literature.
Classification: LCC E873 .R528 2016 | DDC 973.926092--dc23
LC record available at http://lccn.loc.gov/2015042500

Teacher Created Materials

5301 Oceanus Drive
Huntington Beach, CA 92649-1030
http://www.tcmpub.com

ISBN 978-1-4938-2561-5

© 2017 Teacher Created Materials, Inc.
Printed in China
Nordica.082019.CA21901024

8

22

Table of Contents

13

The Boy from Plains

"Come inside, son!" Lillian Carter called. She stood on the porch of the family home outside Plains, Georgia. "We have a new postcard. It's from your uncle in the **Navy**!"

Jimmy put down the peanuts he was stacking in a wagon. The peanuts were grown on the Carter farm.

"Yes, ma'am!" Jimmy called. He loved the postcards his uncle sent. They made him dream of traveling the world. Jimmy thought sailors in the U.S. Navy must be the luckiest people anywhere. One day he hoped to join them.

young Jimmy Carter

Jimmy's childhood home

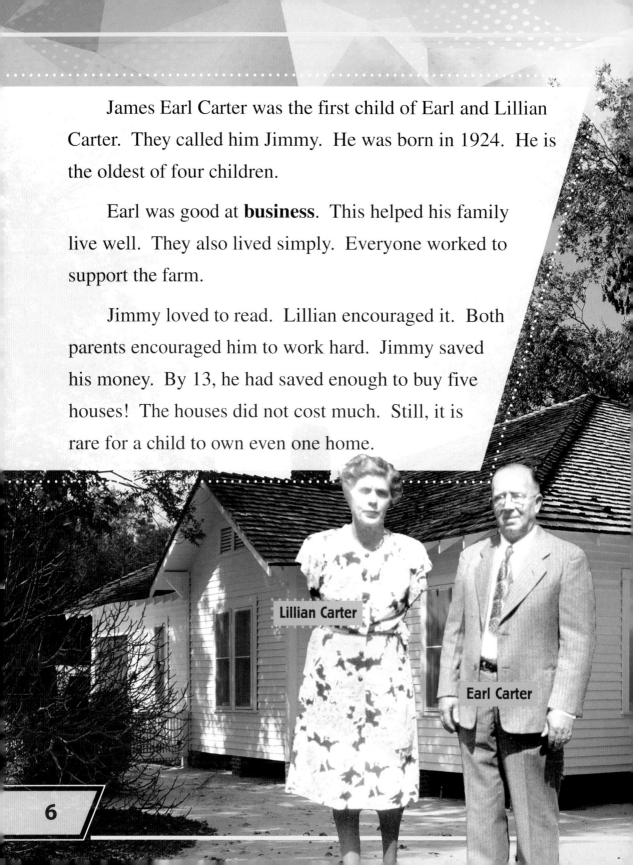

James Earl Carter was the first child of Earl and Lillian Carter. They called him Jimmy. He was born in 1924. He is the oldest of four children.

Earl was good at **business**. This helped his family live well. They also lived simply. Everyone worked to support the farm.

Jimmy loved to read. Lillian encouraged it. Both parents encouraged him to work hard. Jimmy saved his money. By 13, he had saved enough to buy five houses! The houses did not cost much. Still, it is rare for a child to own even one home.

Lillian Carter

Earl Carter

Jimmy stands with his father and his two sisters, Gloria and Ruth.

Future Farmer

In school, Jimmy joined the Future Farmers of America. The group helped him build his farming skills.

Jimmy rides his horse, Lady.

Jimmy's World

Jimmy worked hard and played hard, too. He liked taking care of the animals on the family farm. There were pigs and cows. There were ducks and geese. There were also pets, such as dogs, horses, and guinea (GIHN-ee) hens.

The Carter family was active all the time. They even had a tennis court! Everyone played there. The children were also creative. They made their own toys.

All the children in the family liked to hunt and fish. When they had time, they gathered around the radio. They listened to music, stories, and news.

Jimmy poses with his dog, Bozo.

The world Jimmy could see from his front porch was happy. Simple farm life was all around him.

Jimmy's town was small. Only about 30 families lived there. Most of the people in town were African American. At that time, people of different **races** often did not work and play together. That was not true for Jimmy. All the children worked side by side on the farm. They played side by side, too.

This way of living was the only way Jimmy knew. He would always remember it. He knew this was the right way to live.

Sharecroppers work in a cotton field in 1937.

A 13-year-old sharecropper works in a field in 1937.

Sharecroppers

Sharecroppers rent land from a farmer. They work and live on the land. In return, they share the crops with the land owner. There aren't many crops left over. No one gets rich as a sharecropper.

Jimmy was close to his family. He was also close to a man and woman who rented a cabin on the family farm. They were Jack and Rachel Clark. Jack did chores around the farm. He took care of the barn and mules. Rachel helped on the farm, too. She also helped take care of the Carter children. She was like a second mother to Jimmy.

the Carter family farm

PLAINS
CITY LIMIT

Annie Mae Hollis, the Carter family's nanny, was another important person in Jimmy's life.

Living near Plains taught Jimmy all he needed to know about being a good person. He learned about hard work. He learned about business. And he learned how people should treat one another.

While Jimmy was in high school, a huge war began. It was called World War II. Jimmy wanted to help his country. Joining the U.S. Navy would be a good way to do it.

Jimmy went to college at Annapolis (uhn-NAH-puh-lis). It is a school for Navy students. In 1946, he graduated. He was one of the best students there.

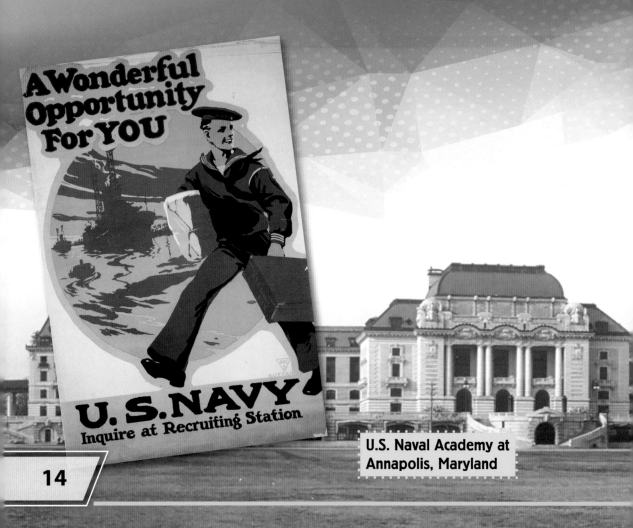

U.S. Naval Academy at Annapolis, Maryland

While in school, Jimmy met a young woman. Her name was Rosalynn Smith. Jimmy wanted to marry her. Rosalynn said no. He asked her again. This time she said yes! They got married right after Jimmy finished school.

Jimmy Carter smiles with his new bride, Rosalynn.

Jimmy and Rosalynn Carter spend time with their sons.

Rosalynn and Jimmy began their life together. Jimmy stayed in the Navy. He worked on submarines. Rosalynn took care of their home and children. They had three boys and then a girl much later.

Jimmy stayed true to his beliefs in his work and life. One time, Jimmy and his submarine crew were docked. All the white members of the crew were invited to a party. The black crew members were not welcome. It was not fair, so Jimmy said he would not go. He asked the others to stay away, too. No one went. Jimmy was a good leader!

Oh, Captain!

Jimmy's captain in the Navy was Hyman Rickover. Jimmy said the captain was his role model.

Hyman Rickover

In 1953, Jimmy's father died. The farm had not been doing well. Jimmy's mother counted on the farm. Jimmy knew what he had to do. He left the Navy. He and his family moved to the farm. Jimmy took his father's place.

A police dog attacks a young man during a protest.

The next years were hard. The farm did not do well. There was a drought. There was also trouble between races. Many white people told Jimmy not to work with African Americans. Jimmy said no. White people would not do business with him. But Jimmy stayed strong. Things slowly changed for the better.

Mr. President

Good business and hard work made the farm a success. They also made Jimmy a leader in his town. Then, they helped him become a state **senator**.

Jimmy liked to serve. But he knew he could do more. He ran for **governor**. He won! But when he gave his first speech, people were surprised. They thought he was like many other people in his **community**. They thought he wanted to keep the races apart. But Jimmy did not. He wanted everyone to work and play together. He wanted all people to have what they needed to live well.

Segregation

Segregation (seg-rih-GAY-shuhn) was common when Jimmy was a young man. He knew it was wrong. He worked hard to stop it.

Jimmy talks to reporters as governor.

Jimmy thought he could do even more to help *all* the people. He wanted a bigger job. He wanted to become president.

People at that time were not happy with the country's leaders. Some poor choices had been made. They wanted a change. Jimmy said he could make the change. The voters thought so, too. They made Jimmy the next president!

The Carters moved into the White House. Rosalynn became a very active first lady. She helped Jimmy do his work. Their daughter, Amy, was the first young child to live in the White House in many years.

White House Cat

Amy's pet cat moved into the White House, too. It was named Misty Malarky Ying Yang.

The next years were tough ones. Jimmy did good work for peace in the world. But there was big trouble in Iran. More than 60 U.S. citizens were taken **hostage** there. Jimmy could not free them.

Jimmy also helped make new laws about energy. But there was an energy crisis, too. Fuel cost a lot, and it was hard to get. People blamed Jimmy for the trouble. They did not elect him for a second **term** as president.

Hostages Released

The hostages in Iran were finally released on the day Jimmy left office.

People wait in line for gas in the 1970s.

Sorry... NO GAS

For the People

Many people agree that Jimmy's best work has been done since he left office. He works for **human rights** and peace. He wants people around the world to be free. He wants them to live well.

Rosalynn and Jimmy visit sick children in Nigeria.

World leaders have often asked Jimmy to help them do tough work. He is an expert in helping people find peace. He also helps the poor. He works to make sure they are treated fairly and have what they need.

Jimmy is a man who is for the people in everything he does.

Middle East Peace

One of Jimmy's biggest successes was helping bring peace to the Middle East. He helped leaders reach important peace agreements. He won the Nobel Peace Prize in 2002.

Sing It!

"Hail to the Chief" was written about 1812. It is the presidential anthem, or song for the president of the United States. Many people know the music but not the words. Learn the words and sing it for your friends and family.

Hail to the Chief we have chosen for the nation,
Hail to the Chief! We salute him, one and all.
Hail to the Chief, as we pledge cooperation
In proud fulfillment of a great, noble call.

Yours is the aim to make this grand country grander,
This you will do, that's our strong, firm belief.
Hail to the one we selected as commander,
Hail to the President! Hail to the Chief!

Glossary

business—the making, buying, and selling of goods or services for money

community—a group of people who live in the same area

governor—the leader of a state or region

hostage—a person who is captured by someone who wants certain things to be done before the captured person is set free

human rights—basic rights that many societies believe every person should have

Navy—a part of the military that is at sea

races—groups of people with common ancestry

segregation—the practice of separating groups of people based on their race or religion

senator—an elected member of the senate who makes laws

sharecroppers—farmers who work on someone else's land for food and shelter

term—length of time

Index

Your Turn!

Inspirational Person

Jimmy Carter noted that Hyman Rickover inspired him. That means that he had a big impact on his life. Think of someone who inspires you. Draw a picture of him or her. Write a short poem that tells how the person inspires you.